Year 2 MATHS (Key stage 1)

National curriculum revision Guide. Targeted revision for multiplication and division word problems.

(Reasoning and problem solving approach)

60 QUESTIONS WITH ANSWER KEY

Created by
Agnes Christy Books
(ACB)

Multiplication and Division
(Reasoning and problem solving)

Year 2 MATHS (Key stage 1)
(Age 6–7)

Word problems

60 questions with answer key

(These word problems will help children to become fluent in the multiplication and division of numbers 1–10 , in addition this improves reasoning and problem solving skills.)

Multiplication Word problems

(Excellent revise guide for year 2 students. These word problems will help children to become fluent in the multiplication of numbers 1–10. Space provided for working out the problem)

1) Molly has 2 sweets in each box. How many sweets will 3 boxes hold?

Ans: [ ]

2)Tony filled 2 bags with apples. He put 4 apples in each bag. How many apples did Tony use?

Ans: [ ]

Work out

3) Esther planted 3 sunflower plants each in the front 5 rows of her garden. How many sunflower plants did Esther plant in her garden?

Ans: ☐

4) Milly bought 3 packs of pens. There were 4 pens in each packet. How many pens did Milly buy?

Ans: ☐

Work out

5) Lily has 3 apples in each bag. How many apples will 2 bags hold?

Ans:

6) Maggie bought 3 packets of pens. There were 4 pens in each packet. How many pens did Maggie buy?

Ans

Work out

7) Len has 3 pens. Amy has 6 times that number. How many pens does Amy have?

Ans: [ ]

8) Mark found 3 packets of biscuits on the table. There was 1 biscuit in each pack. How many biscuits did Mark find?

Ans [ ]

Work out

9) Oliver has 4 pencils in each box. How many pencils will 2 boxes hold?

Ans:

10) Jack bought 3 packets of balloons. There were 5 balloons in each packet. How many balloons did Jack buy?

Ans

Work out

11) Jeff has 5 cakes in each box. How many cakes will 5 boxes hold?

Ans:

12) Gill bought 3 packets of pen. There were 4 pens in each packet. How many Pens did Gill buy?

Ans

Work out

13) Ron made 4 sets of cup cakes. There were 6 cupcakes in each set. How many cup cakes did Ron make?

Ans:

14) Raj bought 7 flowers. Miya has 10 times that number. How many flowers does Miya have? ?

Ans

Work out

15)Thomas planted 2 seeds each in 4 pots. How many seeds did Thomas plant in his pots?

Ans:

16)Cathy bought 3 packets of sweets. There were 5 sweets in each packet. How many sweets did Cathy bought?

Ans:

Work out

17) Linda made 4 sets of bracelets. There were 7 bracelets in each set. How many bracelets did Linda make?

Ans:

18) Maya bought 8 packets of chocolates . There were 8 chocolates in each packet. How many chocolates did Maya buy?

Ans

Work out

19) Jo has 9 books in each box. How many books will 9 boxes hold?

Ans: _____

20) Janet bought 10 packets of beads. There were 9 beads in each packet. How many beads did Janet buy?

Ans _____

Work out

21) Karen made 6 sets of cards for her friend. There were 6 cards in each set. How many cards did Karen make?

Ans: ☐

22) Tom bought 8 packets of marbles. There were 7 marbles in each packet. How many marbles did Tom buy?

Ans ☐

Work out

23) Anna planted 6 seeds each in 7 pots. In total , how many seeds did Anna plant?

Ans: [   ]

24) July bought 6 packets of bangles There were 8 bangles in each packet. How many bangles did July buy?

Ans: [   ]

Work out

25) A house has 3 floors. There are 7 rooms in each floor. How many rooms are there in the house?

Ans: [ ]

26) Maria bought 9 bunches of bananas. There were 7 bananas in each bunch. How many bananas did Maria buy?

Ans: [ ]

Work out

27) James made 9 cakes. There were 4 strawberries on each cake. How many strawberries did James use to make his cakes?

Ans:

28) Riya bought 3 packets of candles. There were 10 candles in each packet. How many candles did Riya buy?

Ans

Work out

29) George has 6 bottles in each box. How many bottles will 9 boxes hold?

Ans:

30) Jane bought 8 packets of pears. There were 4 pears in each packet. How many pears did Janet buy?

Ans

Division
Word
Problems

1) Lina made 18 buns. She arranged them equally on to 3 plates. How many buns were there on each plate?

Ans:

2) Rachel bought 24 rings. She arranged them equally into 6 boxes. How many rings were there in each box?

Ans:

Work out

3) Molly bought 2 boxes of sweets. She had a total of 8 sweets. How many sweets were there in each box?

Ans:

4) Tony bought 8 apples. He arranged them equally on to 4 plates. How many apples did Tony put on each plate?

Ans:

Work out

5) Lily bought apples. 9 of them cost 18 pounds . What was the cost of 1 apple?.

Ans:

6) Milly bought pens. 4 of them cost 12 pounds. What was the cost of one pen?.

Ans

Work out

7) A flat has 50 rooms. There are 10 rooms in each floor. How many floors are there in the building?

Ans: ☐

8) Maria had 56 bananas. There were 8 bananas in each bunch. How many bunches did Maria buy?

Ans: ☐

Work out

9) Lima bought balloon packets. 6 of them cost 18 pounds . What was the cost of 1 balloon packet?

Ans:

10) Daisy bought oranges. 5 of them cost £10. What was the cost of one orange?.

Ans

Work out

11) Sham packed 42 books equally into 7 boxes. How many books were there in each box?.

Ans:

12) 64 children were divided into 8 teams with the same number of children in each team. How many children were there in each team?.

Ans:

Work out

13) 81 pens were tied into bundles of 9 each. How many bundles were made?

Ans: [ ]

14) 35 roses were tied into 7 bunches. How many roses were there in each bunch?

Ans [ ]

Work out

15) 48 seeds were planted equally in 6 rows. How many seeds were planted in each row?

Ans:

16) At a party 54 children were seated equally at 6 tables. How many children sat at each table?.

Ans

Work out

17) Sham packed 42 mangoes equally into 7 boxes. How many mangoes were put in to each box?.

Ans: ☐

18) 45 girls were divided equally into 9 teams. How many girls were in each team?.

Ans ☐

Work out

19) 72 carrots were tied into 9 bundles. Each bundle has the same number of carrots. How many carrots were there in each bundle?

Ans:

20) 36 roses were made into bunches. Each bunch consisted of 6 roses. How many bunches were made altogether?

Ans

Work out

21) Lina made 3 cupcakes. She arranged them equally in 3 boxes. How many cupcakes are there in each box?

Ans:

22) Rodrey bought 40 cakes. He arranged them equally on to 10 plates. How many cakes are there on each plate?

Ans:

Work out

23) A flat has 16 rooms. There are 4 rooms in each floor. How many floors are there in the building?

Ans:

24) Maria had 56 bananas. There were 8 bananas in each bunch. How many bunches did Maria buy?

Ans:

Work out

25) Sam packed 15 cakes equally into 5 boxes. How many cakes were put into each box?.

Ans:

26) 72 sweets were divided equally and put in to 9 bags. How many sweets were there in each bag?

Ans

Work out

27) Sally packed 45 peaches equally into 5 boxes. How many peaches were there in each box?.

Ans:

28) 54 sweets were divided equally and put into 6 bags. How many sweets were there in each bag?

Ans

Work out

29) 32 eggs were used for making 8 chocolate cakes in a factory. How many eggs were used for making one cake?

Ans: _____

30) 49 beads were divided equally to make 7 similar bracelets. How many beads were there in one bracelet ?

Ans _____

Work out

Answer
key
Multiplication

Answer key/Multiplication

1)6
2)8
3)15
4)12
5)6
6)12
7)18
8)3
9)8
10)15
11)25
12)12
13)24
14)70
15)8
16)15
17)28
18)64
19)81
20)90
21)36
22)56
23)42
24)48
25)21
26)63
27)36
28)30
29)54
30)32

Answer
Key
Division

Answer key/Division

1)6
2)4
3)4
4)2
5)2
6)3
7)5
8)7
9)3
10)2
11)6
12)8
13)9
14)5
15)8
16)9
17)6
18)5
19)8
20)6
21)1
22)4
23)4
24)7
25)3
26)8
27)9
28)9
29)4
30)7

All the best for your exam

Created by

Agnes Christy Books
ACB

'Be kind and compassionate to one another.' (Holy Bible)

Printed in Great Britain
by Amazon